WHISH

WHISH

Winner of the Press 53 Award for Poetry

Jackie Craven

Press 53
———•———
Winston-Salem

Press 53, LLC
PO Box 30314
Winston-Salem, NC 27130

First Edition

A Tom Lombardo Poetry Selection

Library of Congress Control Number
2024931884

ISBN 978-1-950413-78-2

*The distinction between past, present and future
is only a stubbornly persistent illusion.*

— Albert Einstein, 1955

CONTENTS

Imaginary time is a new dimension,
at right angles to ordinary, real time.
— Stephen Hawking, 2002

CLOCKS CAN'T BE TRUSTED IN THE ELECTRIC CITY. Imposters stand on every corner, round faces mounted on bronze poles and stone facades. One announces 7:59, another some other time, gonging, gonging with such brass authority that 8:00 A.M. shivers and considers turning back. Between Erie Boulevard and Nott Terrace, a thousand moments, each false as a department store Santa. Cars whish by. Delivery trucks and the Crosstown Express. Groggy passengers gaze through frosted windows. The driver blinks at his watch, which claims to be 8:32. The bus blurs past the transit stop; the forgotten hour waits, smelling of coffee and lavender shampoo.

∞

THE RED LINE RUMBLES AT THE GATEWAY STATION. Whistles screech. Chrome turnstiles spin and squeal. Impatient moments jostle toward departing trains.

In the cacophony, 9:00 A.M. might go unnoticed except for the uncanny resemblance to 9:00 P.M. They are spades and clubs, flip heads on a poker card. In a moment of electromagnetic refraction, the doppelgängers pause, exchange glances, and scurry to their separate appointments.

∞

MANAGEMENT HAS HIRED THREE NEW SECONDS but they mangle every task. One flutters through ceiling vents, one twiddles with the computer fans, one calibrates the world's erratic rotation and jams the copy machine. Bookkeepers whisper about Pulse Frequency Drift. The coffee curdles. Management shrugs — adds a jiffy and a zeptohour. I slump at my desk and pretend the day is round.

∞

FEDERATION AGENTS ASK
WHETHER I'VE EVER BEEN MARRIED,

and I have, but only a little bit, so brief
it's easy to dismiss,
like when you drop a blueberry and quickly snatch it up.
Such a silly slip up (blink and you'd miss it)
yet there's my married name, a tumble of *p*'s and *w*'s
cascading from Deep Space Nine.
It was the price of anchovies
that messed us up, karaoke and pickleball,
the in-laws messed us up, testosterone
messed us up, wormholes, causality loops, and the war,
everywhere garden pests
and tesseracts, and why hold on
to a floppy wedding veil?
I gave the gown to a civic playhouse,
thought I'd moved on, but now investigators
from the Temporal Integrity Commission
demand a name I almost forgot, and that dress,
that ridiculous charmeuse dress,
steps center stage,
a walking shadow reciting Shakespeare —
What's done cannot be undone —
Oh my goodness, I'm wading barefoot in blueberries,
so small, so indelible.

∞

ON EVERY DESK, PAPERS TUMBLE IN PILES, not read, not filed, because 9:22 works on a novel, a sprawling one like the Russians used to write, with wars and summer homes by the sea, and hopeless love, the kind of book that hovers on the *New York Times* bestseller list and teachers never assign because the pages churn with misery and sex. Someone will be loyal and someone betrayed. There will be a garden, a train, a waiting room, a waning moon. Someone will die too young. 9:22 has already collected all the best words and only needs to put them in order.

∞

2:00 A.M. JOLTS AWAKE IN THE DINING CAR of a jostling train. Morning spills through clearstory windows. A coffee urn shrills. The train has passed through the darkest hours and 2:00 A.M. slept through them all. Over the intercom, a metronome announces missed opportunities. Rumpled passengers swirl powdered cream into cardboard cups. Nestled in a bread basket: a nimble-fingered arachnid. When 2:00 asks for directions, she waves a downy arm, unfurls a web of tangled tracks.

∞

LONG BEFORE PERIWINKLES APPEAR, I HOE MY LIFE INTO TIDY ROWS.

1. Radiators hiss and sing of dividends. Ordinary or exceptional?

2a. Taxes due — my father turns 92. He dozes in his swivel chair, feet swollen with deductions, exemptions, and photocopies of my mother's obituary.

4b. The clock itemizes. My father's desk bows beneath depreciated Hallmark cards. I plow through sepia folders, stirring penalties and the scent of expired cigars.

10c. Time runs out. My father struggles over Form 6251. How can a minimum have an alternative?

11g. Calculations lean and topple. Neighbors arrive with cupcakes and songs. Shall I estimate my losses, demand an adjustment? How do we declare benefits we haven't received?

17. Time runs out into the courtyard. Our neighbors call — *Come blow the candles* —

24. Crocuses suck through mud. A weeping cherry weeps its wings. Time depletes and tarantulas scratch at our door. My mother telephones from her grave.

∞

A CLOCK LIVES INSIDE
MY LOOKING GLASS —
stealthy, silver, and synchronized.

I touch her nose. She tips her head.

She glints along the beveled edge
and presses her hand to the shine.

But, you're not real, I cry,
and she breathes, Of course I am,
and softly chimes the hour.

∞

5:00 A.M. PINGS ON MY BEDSIDE TABLE, pings as I grope for silence, pings even as I swat last night's magazine against the window because I mistake 5:00 for a wasp drilling in. The magazine cannot smash 5:00 A.M., but the glass — All those shards ringing to the floor, each bright point spinning toward me while my husband snores from the far side of the galaxy.

∞

NEARLY 10:00 SPRAWLS ON THE PHOTO -COPY MACHINE AND TRIES TO REP- LICATE. Management demands multiple copies coupled with 9:59, 9:58 — all the minutes since daybreak — wedged in leather binders. The copy machine grunts and thrashes. The droning hour presses to the platen glass and pleads for more —

∞

NEARLY 10:00 SPRAWLS ON THE PHOTO -COPY MACHINE AND TRIES TO REP- LICATE. Management demands multiple copies coupled with 9:59, 9:58 — all the minutes since daybreak — wedged in leather binders. The copy machine grunts and thrashes. The droning hour presses to the platen glass and pleads for more —

∞

NEARLY 10:00 SPRAWLS ON THE PHOTO -COPY MACHINE AND TRIES TO REP- LICATE. Management demands multiple copies coupled with 9:59, 9:58 — all the minutes since daybreak — wedged in leather binders. The copy machine grunts and thrashes. The droning hour presses to the platen glass and pleads for more —

∞

I watch from the corridor, a potted plant.

∞

A WILTED BOOKKEEPER HOVERS OVER THE ANTHURIUM and strokes her foliage. Him with his cotton swabs. Him with his coconut spray. He polishes valentine leaves; fondles the fleshy spires. The copy machine moans and the office clock sighs a sad, circular tune.

∞

DOESN'T LOVE HAVE AN EXPIRATION DATE?

— asks a lady at Circle K.
Vapor rises around her face.
Her pale hands hold a carton of eggs.

The milk I purchased already smells off
and along the highway I ponder the problem
of specters who linger too long
and turn sour.

A seatbelt alarm goes *wah-wah-waaaah*
because my blue Subaru
mistakes a gallon jug on the passenger seat
for my husband.

I'd buy a new car, but he's still in this one,
crooning through the broken radio,
every note off-key.

∞

HALF PAST YESTERDAY HAS ABANDONED ME. I sulk in the rain-slicked plaza outside the computer repair shop and the delinquent hour doesn't come. Wind grips my umbrella; sleet stings my face. Half Past Yesterday doesn't call, email, or text. Telephone wires sag with crows too sodden to fly. The fleeting moment flies off to some island where mollusk shells lay thick as peanut brittle. Pining for Noon. Always pining for Noon. I slog through puddles, a statue learning to walk.

∞

2:00 A.M. BLUNDERS INTO THE DAMP CITY, topples garbage pails and collides with morning commuters. Mud sprays from the highway. The lost hour collapses on a bench beside the blur of 9:00 P.M. The stone eagles at City Hall huddle beneath the shush and a colossal clock hiccups in the tower. 2:00 trembles; 9:00 wails.

∞

ALONE IN HER ROOM, THE HUMAN CLOCK CHITTERS AND HUMS. Walls vibrate with gnashing gears, each one sharp as a baby's tooth. Half girl, half machine, she eats shadows in bed. So much artistry went into her construction — Tweezers trembling in swaying light, the ceiling fan gasping *careful, careful*, a laser beam weaving intricate intestinal springs. I want to crack her door and touch the edge of her secrets. All those wires — coiled and cinched into durable knots.

∞

SOMEONE SHOULD DO SOMETHING
ABOUT THE CLOCK AT CITY HALL.

The way it coughs and wheezes, the historic timepiece
can't hold on. Soon megalodons will swim into the harbor
and swallow the paddleboats. We need to help
our heritage clock. The rusty hands can't control
what happens next. Pterodactyls collide with flights
from Baltimore, parasols explode in martinis.
Forget your investments in United Air. Tick after tock,
our beautiful clock turns feverish. Already the rain smells
like watermelons. Our landmark clock loses time
and can't manage the heavy labor of making more.
Lovers who mistreated you will rise like totem poles,
hands in pockets, fingering keys they expect
to still fit your door. Isn't there a cure?
Isn't there a vaccination? Waiting on your porch —
the yellow cat you euthanized. You drink again.
Light a cigarette. Every year on your seventh birthday,
you wet your pants all over again.
After the hardships this clock has endured for us,
don't tell me it's too old to be saved.

∞

NOON STALLS IN THE CENTER OF ERIE BOULEVARD, ignores the caterwauling of trucks and cars. Someone has painted the pavement to show where to cross, but who could follow such a straight path? The earth wobbles on its axis. Shopping carts drift through parking lots. Pigeons ruffle and swerve a lopsided ellipsis. Noon dithers, does not budge — traffic backs up for miles.

∞

8:00 A.M. BROODS BENEATH A GRAY UMBRELLA. Puddles ripple with the patter of quectoseconds, falling, falling more quickly than light. Afternoon drips heavily into dusk. Toyotas swim past, and Teslas, but where's the morning bus?

∞

THE RED LINE RUMBLES AT THE GATEWAY STATION and luggage refuses to board. Knapsacks, carpet bags, and khaki-colored trunks wrench from their leather straps. Clasps break. Carry-ons fall open. Shovels fly out. Spoons and kettles and an oak tree rapping knuckled roots. Cotton underthings billow overhead. Wheeled totes careen through the concourse dragging porcelain dolls. Name tags loop around buckles — pocket watches escape rattling their heavy chains. Brazil and Haiti run away. Entire continents vanish into the crowd. Arresting officers press their knees into resistant duffels and strange bright fruit tumbles out. Hours, days, and centuries in this terminal. Wheels still keen.

∞

SIRENS SHRILL AND FLASH,
heartbeats shake the walls,
and I dream of canaries
who sing in the dark.

My sister sleeps like a giraffe —
neck craned, eyes flickering.
Her doctor calls it nerves, she calls it vigilance.

I remember us as children —
her face in the moonlight,
her gaze fixed on our bedroom door.

I never heard the knob turn.

My sister hasn't slept for 32 years.
Her slippers shush over carpet all through the night.

I don't hear a thing.
I sleep like a log. She sleeps like a dog.
She lets me lie.

∞

WHAT IF HALF PAST YESTERDAY RE-TURNS, giddy as a lottery ticket. What if the prodigal hour tumbles in a gale, hops from a tree, lands on an ephemera table at the flea market in Liberty Park.

Sleet bickers with the sun, clouds gather and break apart. Vendors grumble as they load U-hauls with wares they can't sell. A weary voice mutters, *No one wants Half Past Yesterday anymore.*

I grope my pockets, ready to pay all that I have.

∞

THE RECEPTIONIST REQUISITIONS A GRAVITY BREWER. She wants to turn minutes into hours, but 4:15 is not a coffee bean, will not be steeped, siphoned, or plunged, refuses to drip through a paper filter and pour into mugs embossed with motivational slogans: *This Is Your Moment —*

The rebellious hour whirls through revolving doors — No one, absolutely no one, owns 4:15.

∞

Pi HUDDLES IN A CLOAKROOM beneath scarves and mittens still damp with play. Out in the corridor, children clatter their way to Arithmetic. The teacher has ordered a time-out for Pi, who must learn the obedience of coats on wire hangers.

Thumbtacked to the locked door — a calendar with rows of boxes. Pi must record a month's worth of memories, but February doesn't have enough squares. Moreover, shouldn't memories be round?

Meanwhile in the classroom, students in wooden rows have advanced beyond their years. Already they've discovered how to compute negative square roots and solve problems with imaginary numbers.

The closet smells of crayons and calculus.

$$\infty$$

A BIRD IS MISSING, OR MAYBE A BOOMERANG,
but a blue one fallen from a Calder mobile
so the others hang crookedly, twirling and colliding
when the window fan blows strong.

Their shadows wobble over spoon-shaped chairs
and the sofa where I drowse, a child adrift in the heavy scent
of cocktails and cigarettes.

Dipping and swerving, the shadows become
my father's Thunderbird vanishing over a hill,
then a swirl of phantom birds —

> *Sofa to chair,*
> *chair to sofa,*
> *sofa to chair —*

and the drone of the fan, and my mother
rocking as she moans, *Do you love me?*
Do you love me more than him?

∞

DUSK LANDS ON THE *WHISPERING STATUE,* PAGE 37 — interrupts the moment when Nancy Drew retrieves the waterlogged letter that contains the telltale clue that will lead to the missing husband and a dishonest sculptor. I want to ride with Nancy on rattling trains and crashing seaplanes, but here comes Dusk like a suspicious caller, the likely leader of a ring of thieves.

∞

**MIDNIGHT SHUSHES THROUGH AIR
DUCTS** followed by a whispering stream of hours:
12:26, 1:17, Almost 3:00 — my husband's muffled
voice the evening he slipped through sliding doors,
stood on the patio, and murmured into his phone —

He's gone now, but the refrigerator still whirs —
Trust me. She'll never miss the money.

∞

THE ANTHURIUM RENOUNCES LIFE AS AN ORNAMENTAL OFFICE PLANT. Even as telephones shrill and electric voices shriek *Cash Flow Strategies*, the blossoming epiphyte sprouts strategies of her own. Today she will recoil from tissues, swabs, and fragrance sprays. She will shake off years of undergrowth, polish her own damned self.

Watch her tear up roots. Watch her burst into the fluorescent light of the elevator while the bookkeeper languishes at his desk, breathing carbon dioxide, ozone, and rage.

∞

I'M LEARNING TO BAKE CURSES

the way my mother did
with goddamns and holyshits.
Her recipe book lists fifteen steps
and she's added three more,
her instructions scrawled
on pages brittle as phyllo dough.
I trace my fingers over every fuck
and try to understand the significance
of *Simmer on Low*. I've heard
that if you heat a kettle gently,
a dickhead can't feel the water boil. But
what to do about the grumble
from the dining room, the hungry command
to hurry up? Nothing my mother served
could please my father,
who poured Tabasco into a slow-cooked splooge
and called her a stupid cow.
I lean against the round shoulders
of the old refrigerator and listen
to her murmur. In this scene, I'm grown
and married and I need to know —
When to whisk, when to fold,
when to toss with newts and toads?

∞

HALF PAST YESTERDAY SLEEPS IN MY BED and refuses to be roused. I tuck the sheets tight before I leave for work, but memories muss them up. Slumped at my desk, I can't stop thinking about Half Past Yesterday, who sinks into the mattress and burrows a hollow shaped like a gibbous moon, which has not slept there for years.

∞

63:13 SHIVERS ON THE MARQUEE of Citizens Savings & Loan, a dreary old building made of stones shaped like dollar bills. Throw a penny and there's no clink or echo. The coin vanishes because no one understands or respects 63:13. Soon electricians will come with their tall yellow ladders. When they fix the clock, where will the broken hour go?

63:13 blinks, plots a getaway.

∞

AS HER STEEL FRAME EXPANDS, THE HUMAN CLOCK WRITHES AND TRIES TO SMILE. Fibers ravel at the wrists. *Never mind*, she says, *I'll recalibrate* —

She taps her harmonic oscillator, turns a thumb screw to adjust the rate of vibrations. But what about irregularities in the earth's cycles, caesium atoms bouncing in cavities — *Pulse Frequency Drift?*

Wires spark and screech. *I should have been born with zippers,* she sighs, and tears herself open at the seams.

∞

I ESCAPE TO CAPTIVA ISLAND

only to be pinged by the girl who stole my husband
twenty years ago. She wants to apologize
for anguish I no longer feel and
(she's sorry to inform) he's passed on.
What difference does this make now?
I watch the sun rise. I kick off my sandals
and wade into the tide. Tourists arrive
but no one swims in the serene water.
Silent and swaying, they glide past me on the beach
and scoop scallops and baby's ears with little plastic nets
from the souvenir shop on Periwinkle.
I do not have a net, I could not keep him.
Her eyes were Velcro, her voice spun webs.
My footsteps crunch over sharp exoskeletons
of dead things from the sea.
On a pebbled shore below the causeway,
a fisherman struggles with a snowy egret.
A splot of red on white — The egret
hooked on his line. My shoulder blades hurt
where wings should sprout.
Do I help the fisherman release the bird?
Do I forgive my husband's widow?
Every piece of me wants to crush her skull.

∞

MIDNIGHT BOARDS THE RED LINE, an astonishment on my fingertip, microscopic and huge. Like a thirsty star, like a bristled rambutan, the dark hour bellows, *O mio sospiro e palpito* — *Breath of life you'll be to me.*

Graffiti blurs, numbers flicker forward and back. This train can't reach the terminal without first going halfway, but the train's only halfway to halfway. Midnight winks and offers a seat. I cling to a swaying strap.

∞

5:15 PACES HOSPITAL CORRIDORS and frets over where to hide the secrets. Security cameras hover overhead. 5:15 clings to latex gloves, hijacks medicine carts. Anyone might mistake the stowaway for an erotic floral arrangement. Beaming behind his mask, an orderly carries anthuriums through antiseptic halls to Intensive Care.

∞

WHAT ALIEN ASTRONAUTS FEAR

Not the rasp of dying engines or fiery explosions
or wandering naked through the universe, nor
any of the nightmares that follow me in the
dark. My sister has swallowed pills.

Six hundred trillion miles from Earth, a starship
drifts across the bowl of the Big Dipper. Our
father raises the window blinds. The sky turns
violet; the vessel turns drowsy somersaults.

I don't need a telescope to see extraterrestrials
lean into the light of their monitors, strange
and wooden as totem poles. Why don't they
call for help? Such sad, other-worldly creatures,
each born with only two or three words and
every one essential as a kidney or a lung. Once
spoken, what then?

The reservoir dwindles — the ship loses fuel.
Longevity is a blessing given only to the mute.
When I wake, I see castaways, faces pressed to
portholes, lips stretched tight.

∞

THE DAY *CHALLENGER* EXPLODED
my husband and I were newlyweds
celebrating at a bar on Canaveral Pier.
Mist rose from icy water.
Tourists sipped Piña Coladas with pineapple
and paper flags.

Giddy voices chanted in unison with CNN —
Twenty-one seconds till liftoff.
Or, did the announcer say we're down to twelve?

My husband's lips turned blue in the uncertain morning light.
We didn't know, but already suspected trouble in his cells.
When did he begin to count down?

Life is measured in small subtractions:
T minus this, T minus that —

∞

**HALF PAST NIGHTFALL CLINGS TO THE
SEAWALL INSIDE ME,** a barnacle on my uterus,
only observable when the surgeon inserts a tube
above the navel. Under anesthesia I see a swirl of
blue moons, masked faces leaning close. Shadows
flit across my ocean floor and, beyond cliffs and
canyons, a snore.

∞

3:00 A.M. HOVERS ON A BALCONY suspended between Midnight and Dawn. Feathered trees bow over the Mohawk River and repeat in silver water. The moon sinks into the slough, the slough dreams it's sky, and a surprised-eyed bluegill swims overhead. Two thousand frogs turn the night green. 3:00 A.M. ripples, forgets to breathe.

∞

BEHIND A LOCKED DOOR, THE *SSSS* OF SHALIMAR spritzed from cut glass bottles and at night the hiss of soft skin shedding. For a moment the Human Clock holds her shape, elbows bent and hands folded in the posture she wears at her desk in school. Then she rustles down.

I imagine a perfect pointed toe stepping out, careful not to snag cellulose threads. What does the Human Clock become while she soaks herself in the bathroom sink? Can a girl exist without her skin?

I find her folded over the shower curtain rod, arms dangling, the mask of her face upside down, dripping into the tub.

∞

IN MEMORY'S DARKROOM,
I try to slide what I cannot see
around a slippery spool and would never succeed
if not for the boy who glides so smoothly through our school
with his telephoto lens extended.

Like this, he whispers,
and then the swoosh of film in fluid
and the thump of a basketball
in the gym next door.

I shake the canister too fast.
I shake it too slowly.
What do I know about chemistry, temperature,
or the urgent need for agitation?

His damp hands give off the scent of vinegar
but his voice is syrup —
That's okay. You'll do better next time.
He clicks on lights and cuts the unfurled film
into dripping strips: Limp hair, hollow eyes,
lights and darks reversed.

I'll expose you tomorrow, he says,
and hangs me from the ceiling to dry.

∞

DEXTEROUS AS JORŌ SPIDER, 6:52 swings from my ceiling and shimmies through a series of disguises. *Astronaut. Butterfly. Giraffe.* When I look at 6:52, I see my sister's face. I brew the lavender tea she loves. Strains of Puccini rise from the kettle. Misery steams in our cups.

∞

EVENING CREEPS INTO THE ROOTS OF OUR FATHER'S HAIR. He claims he never turned gray, but I found deception on his bathroom shelf. Before he died, our father bought a catamaran. Snapshots show him reclined on the deck, shirt open to display a pelt of curls too dark to be real. Even the setting sun seems suspect, the way it gilds the surface of Buzzards Bay, glints on the chain around his neck, and sizzles into the rising fog.

In the distance, a craggy knoll,
a dim lighthouse,
the furtive glow—

∞

TELEVISIONS GLIMMER IN HOSPITAL WAITING ROOMS. Even as a hound bays out on the moor, they speak of extraterrestrials who save on groceries every day. I'm free to fly the fragrant skies or sleep beneath murmurs that drift — softly, softly — from Cardassia Prime.

Their voices are blue and absorb like magic. They say one replicator outperforms a thousand microwaves; they promise to guard the hyperdrive. But where's my witness?

In the criminal justice system, there's another dimension. Anthropods may exhibit changes in behavior, thinking, mood. On Starship Enterprise, they howl and howl.

∞

MY MISERY SLEEPS THROUGH SUNRISE.
Nothing can rouse her,
not the revelry of sparrows in the eaves,
not the blush of light on our bedroom wall
or the sultry aroma rising
from the mug I bring.
I've been up for hours,
brewing coffee, jingling spoons,
and Misery lies in twisted sheets,
comforter crumpled on the floor.
She listens to her clock radio—
Glaciers weep, pathogens carouse,
and in Martha's Vineyard, manatees
wash ashore. I smooth her sheets
and fold hospital corners, every crease
a lumbering disappointment. I'm a manatee
making origami and Misery's a pillow
stuffed with sparrows, plush
and nettlesome. They warble beneath
the weight of burning ice. Polar bears
sit on her chest. For only $9 a month
we can save a polar bear but
can we afford to restore the world?
One doomed eye creaks open. *Let's.*
Just like that: *Let's*, and my lungs
swell with feathers.

∞

NOON IDLES ON ERIE BOULEVARD and searches for shadows. The sun glowers down. Gold teeth glint from the cornice of the Savings & Loan, but the bank casts no shadow. The bronze statue of Thomas Edison freezes in a pool of light. Hours drain from the pale face in the clock tower at City Hall.

∞

63:13 LODGES IN MY SISTER'S FRONTAL LOBE and lands in the center of her speech and executive function just as she returns home with more pineapples than any one person should carry. A watermelon bursts through her paper sack followed by a bundle of anthuriums and seven eggs. Yolks slide across porcelain tiles. Someone shouts, *Jesus, look what you've done.* Tottering to her knees, my sister mistakes our father's irritated voice for 63:13. She struggles to reply; her own voice breaks.

∞

URGENT CARE HAS NO TIME FOR US. A
poster on the wall explains: Breath, once exhaled,
expels time. Now there's not enough.

Gravity scuttles across linoleum floors, lapping
minutes as they fall.

∞

WHEN HER TONGUE BREAKS
THE HUMAN CLOCK TRIES TO SAY:

They put me in I want. You to know they put. Is you vay cay tion. Put me onetwothree. One nay tion. I want you to know. One two station. They put me in ice long. Do you know they put me in salve-ation. Is you know they put. I so you to know they put me in. Sixseven nay-tion. So long they put. Onetwo four I want. You to know they put me in I so lay tion. They put. I want.

∞

**JUST FOR ONCE, I WANT TO WITNESS
THE GOING AWAY.** I want to catch the moment,
cup it in my hands, see it blink like an altar candle.
But in this dream, the Red Line shrieks from the terminal
hours before I arrive. Or I reach Port Canaveral
after the Boatswain's final call. I'm alone on the pier,
waving goodbye, waving come back, waving
until my watch slides from my wrist
and tumbles into the foaming wake. I'm so thirsty —
thirsty the way my father must have been
in his hospice bed. I dab his mouth
with a moist sponge. I tell him, Here I am,
I'm right here. And so I am,
except I turn to read the clock. I miss
the instant he leaves. The Timex watch
my mother gave me in high school
tsks from the floor of the harbor —
Can't you be quicker? —
and I hear my husband tick.
My sister lies on the kitchen floor.
I pinch her nose, push air through her lips,
yet I don't see her whish out to her garden,
midnight dark and flecked with fireflies.
I can never move fast enough —

∞

11:59 SLUMPS ON A STOOL AT THE CORNER CAFÉ.
Coffee chills in heavy mugs. A couple gazes vacantly at the white-clad waiter who clatters behind the counter. Was there ever a time before now? Will the chipped hands of the wall clock inch past this moment?

The bleary window, the empty street, the static air — Salvador Dalí might have painted this scene. 11:59 cannot move forward or back, cannot imagine a world beyond the frame.

∞

2:02 GIVES UP HOOVES, abandons farm and field for neon shoals. Swirling through plankton thick as phlegm, 2:02 sinks into hush and shriek.

Squid. Spotted eels. Whales grazing on kelp and krill.

Five hundred million years below bubble and froth, boneless bodies pillow on the fossil floor. 2:02 slides beneath the green, descends like Atlantis when Atlantis let go of air.

∞

PRESERVED IN A BASEMENT CLOSET, fragments from the Human Clock sorted into rubber bins and coffee tins. *My god,* how to make sense of her hour hands and winding keys, the resin eyes and quartz suspension wires, so many pulleys and chains, and, drooping from hat hooks along the wall, the translucent membranes she stretched and shed, each one sheer as a butterfly net.

In her quiet way, the Human Clock told me she longed to fly. A cellophane package on the shelf holds neon wings large enough to hoist a full-grown woman. I'd try them on, but she left a fastidious note: *Save for later.*

∞

UNDER ANESTHESIA I REMEMBER
A MOON WITH SLIPPERY SEEDS —

My sister and I sit on our mother's stoop
    and spit seeds into the tall grass.

Pulp clings to our fingers.
    Bumblebees tangle in our hair.

We spit across the lawn to our father's
    garden shed.

Somewhere from the future, a surgeon says
    God what a mess.

His voice rumbles. A lawnmower
    begins to roar.

Crickets shriek up from chickweed.
    Petals swirl through linoleum halls.

Quick, my sister says, do this —
    We bury seeds in the fevered soil.

∞

HALF PAST TOMORROW SLUMBERS IN THE REAR OF THE FREEZER, wrapped in plastic and clinging to a gray side of beef, not desired but saved, and why? I've moved to a new house, a new job, a new lover. Still, there's Half Past Tomorrow, a drowsy glacier in a swirl of arctic steam, crystalizing and thawing in the light from the door I left open.

∞

DAWN DREAMS A NEW UPENDING. A male truck idles at the curfew. My bruise-paper molders on the porch. Already children trudge up the pill to their elementary scheme. I rub my sighs and put coffins on to brew. If only I were yogurt! Dawn announces a new pretending. Hours scuttle from shadows; minutes quiver into human shapes. Bobbing beneath damp umbrellas, they chase buses through fog and freezing pain. If it weren't for the chills, I'd quit my throb. The day unveils anxious faces. Hurried seconds flutter their wings. I wonder if I'll have enough ink to carry on. I cheat my toast and rush to worry, pushing 75, 80. Years rattle in my briefcase. Watches call my name.

∞

THE RESCUE MISSION WANTS TO KNOW IF I STILL HAVE HIS OLD CLOTHES. I've already folded my husband's possessions into thirty gallon bags meant for garbage but just right for the satin-striped slacks he wore to the swing dance festival while a roast smoldered in the oven. I never asked who gave him the white poplin Armani that had no buttons only pearl-topped snaps that made popping sounds nights he undressed in the dark room where I pretended to sleep. *I was a loving wife,* I tell his empty closet and cinch the sack with a practiced Windsor knot.

∞

AS THE LAST EGG IN THE CARTON,
I SHOULD TELL YOU ABOUT THE OTHERS:

#1 beat phantom wings against the walls of her shell.

#2 dreamed her shell turned into a pearl.

#3, 4, and 5 churned their dreams into boasts.
Each claimed to hold the biggest yolk.

My yolk is huge and made of light.

At the rear of the carton, a runt imagined himself a cock
and bullied the sun.

Whoosh — Another gone.

Ghosts drift across a frozen moon.

Can a moon really rise inside a refrigerator?

I am large and bright, very bright, and too smart to disappear.

∞

1:00 A.M. CAN'T SEE 1:00 A.M. IN MIRRORS.
Mirrors reflect the tile wall, the shower curtain, the toilet, but never 1:00. In the hollow of a windowless room, the hypnotic drip of a faucet. Water appears transparent, but turns turquoise in the tropical sun. Moments pass as I grope along the wall, find the switch. What appears in a flash is not 1:00, not 1:00 at all, but some other time, who also leans into the mirror —

∞

1:00 A.M. CAN'T SEE 1:00 A.M. IN MIRRORS.
Mirrors reflect the tile wall, the **medicine cabinet**, the
toilet, but never buried thoughts. In a windowless
room, the **seductive** drip of a faucet. Water **cannot
reflect** while it rushes toward the **Caribbean Sea**.
Moments pass as I grope along the wall, find the
switch. What appears in a flash is **not me, not me**
at all, but an **alternate** who also leans into
the mirror—

∞

63:13 RAPS AT MY DOOR and claims to be Half Past Tomorrow. I want to believe this. I arrange anthuriums in a vase on the credenza and my sister's ghost follows, sweeping up the rust. She knows the broken hour is an imposter. No rational person would mistake 63:13 for an actual time. But what's the harm?

The anthuriums are replicas, and the credenza, too. Everything in our house, down to the framed portrait of Half Past Tomorrow, imitates something that the broken hour spirited away. My sister offers to call the police, but what good would that do? We are replicas, too.

∞

SONNET WITH 8 LEGS

What if Time lives in your cellar, [8] has always
lived in your cellar, [16] spinnerets unfurling glass
strings [24] — your youth stretched beam to beam,
marriage [32] swinging by a thin breath — while
Time, [40] eight-legged, eight-eyed aerialist, [48]
hurtles from joist to laundry tub, [56] snags earwigs,
sowbugs, and squabbles, [64] every petulant word
you said, [72] and saves them for later. Years
wrapped [80] in limp and sticky bundles, but [88]
try to sweep away the debris [96] and Time clings to
your broom, twitching, [104] lockstitching threads
you never

∞

SOMEONE MOVED THE BAGEL SHOP,
took down the cell tower, rearranged the trees,
the temple-shaped savings & loan —
even the signs have changed their names
as though roads I trusted ran off
and married a real estate developer
who converts churches into condominiums.
Turn right, says my dead husband, whose spirit
I've conjured in our dark car, so I do,
and Erie Boulevard becomes a thin blue line,
tangles at the fold
and unfurls from a hollow dot that might be Brigadoon
fading into the mist, or
the town where I lived before we met—
Not here, he says, *There — Can't you see?* —
but I see only a billboard, a looming reminder to pray,
which I do,
groping for that psalm about the shepherd—
Lead me to still waters —
until the words slip away
and I'm alone on a byway,
headlights blinking.

∞

I'M SPEEDING THE QUANTUM HIGHWAY, pushing 75, 80 — Radio towers lose their grip, songs flutter from rap to gospel. I whish along the Quantum Highway, move so quickly I stand still — I can never move fast enough. I'm speeding on the Quantum Highway and I'm in a chapel with a small black box, tightly clasped to hold cremains that meow and scratch to escape. I'm whooshing over the Quantum Highway and the dust that was my mother plumes into the stained glass light, or maybe it's my father or my sister, my husband and so many friends —

I carry them in my lungs, under my fingernails, and on the soles of my shoes, track them up carpeted stairs to a room still painted the green shade of blue I loved as a child. I throw back the sheets only to find myself already there. I'm speeding the Quantum Highway and I sit beside the bed where I sleep, guarding the door, making sure I don't slip away —

∞

NOTES

Epigraphs

— Albert Einstein, in a letter of condolence to the family of his beloved friend and colleague, Michele Besso, who died in March 1955. Einstein died the following month. In English, the passage is often translated to read: "Now he has departed from this strange world a little ahead of me. That means nothing. People like us, who believe in physics, know that the distinction between past, present, and future is only a stubbornly persistent illusion." The letter in the original German with a French translation appears in *Correspondence, 1903-1955*, Albert Einstein (author), Michele Besso (author), Pierre Speziali (translator). (Paris: Hermann, 1972)

— Stephen Hawking, quoted by Gregory Benford, "Leaping the Abyss," (*Reason Magazine*, April 2002)

Page 3, "Management has hired three new seconds"

Because of variations in the earth's rotation, a solar day is usually a little shorter than 24 hours. The discrepancy adds up, so every so often "leap seconds" are added. These adjustments are imperfect and can cause technical mishaps and scheduling snafus. In November 2022, a coalition of scientists and government agencies voted to abolish the practice, effective 2035.

Page 4, "Federation agents ask whether I've ever been married"

Deep Space Nine was a *Star Trek* television series with episodes that included wormholes, temporal anomalies, and an intergalactic federation with a Department of Temporal Investigations.

(Page 4, cont)

The Shakespeare quote is spoken by Lady Macbeth in *Macbeth*, Act 5, scene 1.

Page 6, "2:00 A.M. jolts awake in the dining car"

In *Metamorphoses,* Ovid tells the ancient Greek myth of Arachne, who excelled at weaving. Enraged by the maiden's hubris, the goddess Athena transformed Arachne into a spider.

Page 23, "Pi huddles in a cloakroom"

Pi, or π, is the ratio of a circle's circumference to its diameter. Pi cannot be expressed by a simple fraction. After the decimal point, the digits extend infinitely.

"Imaginary numbers" are seemingly impossible numbers which, when squared, turn negative. Imaginary numbers help solve real-life equations and may provide essential information for experiments in quantum physics.

Page 33, "Midnight boards the Red Line"

The Greek philosopher Zeon of Elia (c. 490 – 430 BC) developed a series of paradoxes, or mind puzzles, to challenge laws of physics. One paradox proposed that any moving object must reach a halfway point before arriving at its destination. Since there's always the need to go half the distance, no destination can be ever reached.

Notes

Page 36, "The day *Challenger* exploded"

The space shuttle *Challenger* launched from Cape Canaveral, Florida on January 28, 1986 and exploded at 11:39 EST, just 73 seconds after liftoff, killing the entire crew, including high school teacher Christa McAuliffe.

Page 43, "Televisions glimmer in hospital waiting rooms"

In the *Star Trek* television series, Cardassia Prime was a dark, humid planet where disease and famine lead to military rule and uprisings from the oppressed.

Page 61, "Sonnet with 8 legs"

The numbers indicate syllable counts — 8 syllables for each phrase, except for the closing phrase, where the final syllable is missing.

Page 63, "I'm speeding the Quantum Highway"

During a discussion with Albert Einstein, physicist Erwin Schrödinger devised a thought experiment to illustrate concepts of quantum superposition. Schrödinger suggested that a cat in a closed box might be considered simultaneously dead and alive, as long as it is not observed.

ACKNOWLEDGMENTS

Thank you to the editors of the following publications, in which versions of these poems first appeared.

AGNI: "A bird is missing," originally titled "Under a Calder Mobile, August 1959"

Alaska Quarterly Review: "Federation agents ask whether I've ever been married," originally titled "Social Security Asks Whether I've Ever Been Married"

Beloit Poetry Journal: "My misery sleeps through sunrise," originally titled "Morning Unmoors Us"

Chautauqua: "Someone moved the bagel shop," originally titled "Dysgeographica"

Cleaver: "Dawn dreams a new upending," originally titled "Auto Corrected"

Cola Literary Review: Excerpts from "Half Past Yesterday," "Half Past Nightfall," and "Half Past Tomorrow" published under the title "Half Past 11:00"

Dark House: "Doesn't love have an expiration date?" originally "7-Eleven Blues" in the anthology titled, What We Talk about When We Talk About It: Variations on the Theme of Love, Vol. 1

Mayday Magazine: "The day Challenger exploded," originally titled "Clear Skies, Unseasonably Cold"

New Ohio Review: "I'm learning to bake curses," originally titled "Cursing Lessons"

Pleiades: "The Red Line rumbles at the Gateway Station (and luggage refuses to board)," originally titled "Surveillance Video Shows Suitcases Resisting Arrest"; Passages from several of the "Human Clock" poems are adapted from a single short poem titled "Cyborg Sister"

Ploughshares: "Just for once, I want to witness the going away" and "I'm speeding the Quantum Highway" adapted from a single poem titled "Whish"

Red Eft Review: "Long before periwinkles appear," originally titled "Many Happy Returns"

River Styx: "I escape to Captiva Island," originally titled "Captiva Island" (International Poetry Contest runner-up); "What alien astronauts fear" (International Poetry Contest Honorable Mention)

Rogue Agent: "Under anesthesia I remember a moon with slippery seeds," originally titled "Under Anesthesia, I Remember a Watermelon with Slippery Seeds"

Salamander Magazine: "The anthurium renounces life as an ornamental office plant," adapted from a poem titled "I Renounce My Life as a Philodendron"

Stone Canoe: "The Rescue Mission wants to know if I still have his old clothes," originally titled "The Lupus Society Wants to Know if I Have Old Clothes for Their Collection"; "Televisions glimmer in hospital waiting rooms," originally titled "Televisions in Hospital Waiting Rooms"

Vine Leaves Press: 50 Give or Take Anthology, "Nearly 10:00 sprawls on the photocopy machine," originally titled "Minutes Have Souls"

///

Special thanks to the editors of Headmistress Press for publishing *Cyborg Sister*, a finalist in the Charlette Mew competition. Versions of "Dusk lands on the *Whispering Statue*, page 37," "Under Anesthesia I Remember," and portions of "The Human Clock" poems are adapted from that chapbook.

Thank you also to *Speculative North Magazine* for reprinting the short poem that grew into several of the Human Clock poems.

And, many thanks to the judges of the DiBiase Poetry Contest for awarding and reprinting "Whish," a short poem that evolved into "Just for once, I want to witness the going away" and "I'm Speeding the Quantum Highway."

///

The organization and focus of this collection would not have been possible if not for feedback from many fine writers in my local poetry community.

For daily inspirations, I am indebted to Susan Carroll Jewell.

For shepherding the manuscript into the world, I am deeply grateful to Press 53, most especially to my editor Tom Lombardo and publisher Kevin Morgan Watson.

Jackie Craven writes poetry and prose steeped in magical realism. Her previous books include *Secret Formulas & Techniques of the Masters* (Brick Road Poetry Press, 2018) and chapbooks from Headmistress Press and Omnidawn. Recent poems have appeared in *AGNI*, *Alaska Quarterly Review*, *The Cincinnati Review*, *Ploughshares*, and many other journals and anthologies. She holds a Doctor of Arts from the English Department at the University at Albany, NY and lives in Schenectady where she hosts a long-standing open mic for writers. Find her at JackieCraven.com

Cover artist Sharon Craven Kinzer (1943-2022) became known for her intricate *trompe l'oeil* paintings. She studied classical techniques at the Schuler School of Fine Arts in Baltimore and exhibited her work at the Smithsonian Institute, Veerhoff Gallery in Washington D.C., and many other museums and galleries. She grew up in Virginia with her sister (the author) and their artist mother, and lived in Ohio and North Carolina with her husband and sons. Paintings can be viewed at SharonCravenKinzer.com

9 781950 413782